DRESSING WITH PRIDE

MARÍA
HERMINIO ACUÑA
AND
MALY NY

PHOTOGRAPHY BY
DARREN YOKOTA

Rigby

00 99 98 97 96
10 9 8 7 6 5 4 3 2 1

Printed in the United States of America

ISBN 0-7635-3158-8

Clothes are an important way of showing who we are. By wearing traditional clothing, Asian Americans honor their culture and show where they came from. Because the children in this book are growing up in the United States, the clothes they wear for school are usually like those of other American children. They are Asian and American, just like their clothes.

Meet Tiffany and Theresa Nguyen. Their parents came from Vietnam to the United States in 1988. Tiffany and Theresa were born here. Theresa is in second grade and loves math. Tiffany is just three years old and loves to help her mother cook Vietnamese food.

Tiffany and Theresa pose with their father. The girls are wearing traditional clothes called *Ao Dai*. These clothes are made of silk or satin and are worn over wide pants. The girls wear Ao Dai for weddings, New Year celebrations, and other special events. Tiffany and Theresa feel very proud when they wear these traditional clothes.

Meet Gina, Mina, and Nancy Chang. Their parents came from Laos to the United States in 1979. The girls were born here. For New Year, the Chang family prepares special foods and wears traditional clothes. Gina, Mina, and Nancy feel very proud when they wear this clothing.

The girls pose with their mother. Laotian women have many types of traditional clothing. All are made with a special Asian silk. Gina is wearing a Laotian dress that covers only one shoulder. Mina and Nancy are wearing clothing and hats from the Hmong culture. The skirts are called *Tab*. In front of the Tab is a longer piece called the *Sev* with sequins and silver coins sewn onto it.

Meet Stacey and Stephanie Chau. Their family came from China to the United States in 1979. The girls were born here. They are twins and are in the third grade. Stephanie enjoys mathematics, and Stacey enjoys sports.

The girls pose with their mother. All three are wearing a traditional Chinese dress called *ch'i-p'ao*. The family keeps their Chinese traditions alive by wearing this dress for Chinese New Year and for special parties. Each dress is made of one close-fitting piece of silk. Like many Chinese women, Mrs. Chau likes to wear red because she believes it brings good luck.

Meet Marina Sos. Marina was just one year old when she came to the United States with her parents in 1980. The Sos family came from Cham, a region of Cambodia that has its own language and culture. One day they would like to return there to visit their family.

Marina poses with her parents. Marina and her mother are wearing a shirt and long skirt. A veil covers their hair. Mr. Sos is wearing a loose-fitting shirt and a *sarong*. The sarong is a kind of skirt wrapped around the waist. The hat he is wearing is called a *katep*. The Sos family wears traditional clothes when they go to their temple. Marina likes to wear jeans and dresses for school. At home, she likes to wear a sarong like her father's since she finds it more comfortable.

11

Meet Khao Sok. Khao was just one year old when he and his family left Cambodia to come to the United States. The most important holiday for the Sok family is New Year. The Cambodian New Year is April 13, and it is celebrated for three days.

Khao poses with his parents. Khao and his father are wearing loose-fitting shirts and baggy pants that wrap around the waist like a sarong. His mother is holding a traditional purse and wearing a silk skirt decorated with a golden design. Khao thinks that his mother looks very pretty when she wears her traditional Cambodian clothes. The Sok family wears these clothes when they go to their temple, and the clothes make them feel very proud.

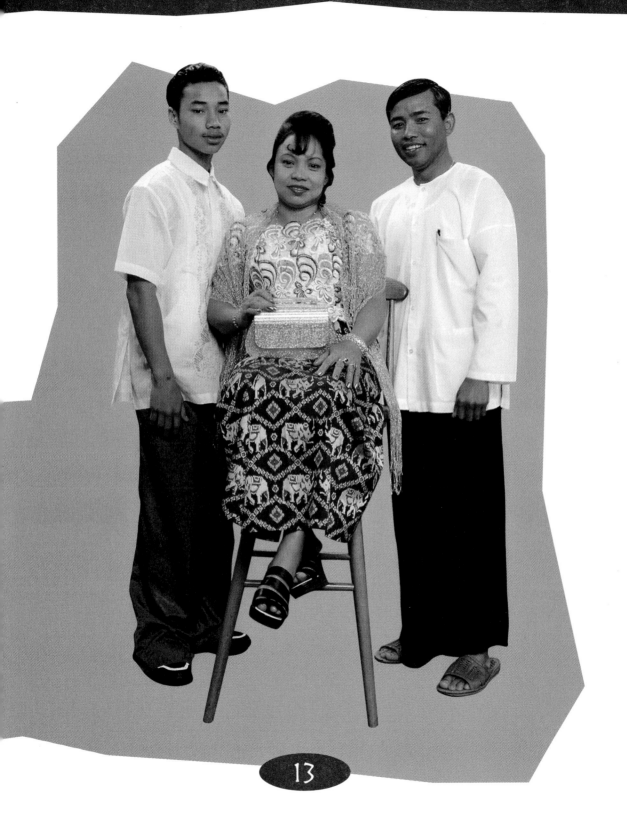

Meet Kaoru and Kiyomi Fukuda. Their father is from Japan, and their mother is from Mexico. They were both born in the United States. Kaoru is nine years old, and Kiyomi is eight. The girls speak three languages: English, Spanish, and Japanese. They go to a special school on Saturdays to learn to read and write Japanese.

The girls pose with their father. Kaoru and Kiyomi are wearing *yukata*, a Japanese lightweight cotton robe worn during warm summer weather. The wooden sandals they are wearing are called *geta*. The girls enjoy wearing their traditional Japanese clothing for special occasions.

Having two different styles of dress is one way these Asian American children express that they are part of two different worlds.

These children share the cultures of the United States, where they live, and Asia, where their families came from.

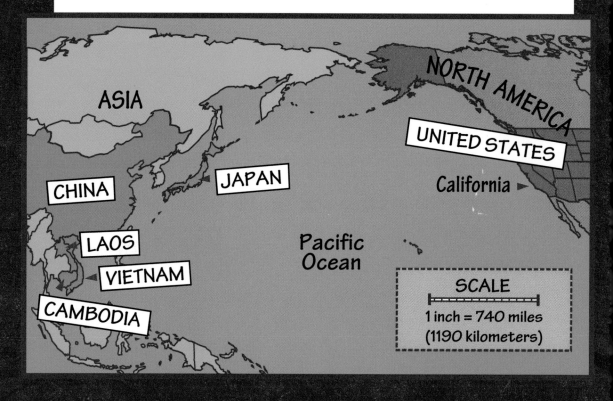

ASIA

NORTH AMERICA

UNITED STATES

CHINA

JAPAN

California ▶

LAOS

VIETNAM

Pacific Ocean

CAMBODIA

SCALE

1 inch = 740 miles
(1190 kilometers)